AnimalWays

Turtles

AnimalWays

Turtles

REBECCA STEFOFF

Marshall Cavendish
Benchmark
New York

With thanks to Dr. Dan Wharton, director of the Central Park Wildlife Center, for his expert reading of this manuscript.

Marshall Cavendish Benchmark
99 White Plains Road
Tarrytown, NY 10591-9001
www.marshallcavendish.us

Library of Congress Cataloging-in-Publication Data

Stefoff, Rebecca,
Turtles / by Rebecca Stefoff.
p.cm.–(Animalways)
Summary: "An exploration of the life cycle, diet, behavior, anatomy, and conservation status of turtles"– Provided by publisher.
Includes bibliographical references and index.
ISBN 978-0-7614-2539-7
1.Turtles--Juvenile literature. 1. Title.
QL666.C5S767 2007
597.92--dc22
2007013178

Publisher: Michelle Bisson
Art Director: Anahid Hamparian

Photo research by Candlepants Incorporated

Cover Photo: age fotostock / Super Stock

The photographs in this book are used by permission and through the courtesy of:
Corbis: Raymond Gehman, 2, back cover; David A. Northcott, 12, 67, 69; Bettmann, 15; Frank Lane Picture Agency, 18; Joe McDonald, 23, 73, 74(lower); Kevin Schafer, 45; DK Limited, 49; Maurizio Lanini, 55; Kennan Ward, 63; Anthony Bannister; Gallo Images, 70; Martin Harvey, 84; Michael & Patricia Fogden, 90. *AP Images*: Bikas Das, 9. *The Bridgeman Art Library*: Private Collection, 10. *Super Stock*: age fotostock, 24, 64, 72, 87. *Peter Arnold Inc.*: R. Andrew Odum, 28; John Cancalosi, 31; Martin Harvey, 42; Kelvin Aitken, 51, 36; M. Blachas, 59; M. Mavrikakis, 62, 78; Matt Meadows, 74(top); Fred Bruemmer, 95. *Photo Researchers Inc.*: M. Phillip Kahl, 30; Michael Patrick O'Neall, 61; James R. Fisher, 40. *Getty Images*: Jon M. Fletcher, 35; Nicole Duplaix/NGS, 58; Jim Merli, 68. *Minden Pictures*: Georgette Douwma/npl , 60; Pete Oxford, 71; Norbert Wu, 94.

Printed in Malaysia
1 3 5 6 4 2

Contents

Animal Kingdom

CNIDARIANS

coral

ARTHROPODS
(animals with jointed limbs and external skeleton)

MOLLUSKS

squid

CRUSTACEANS

crab

ARACHNIDS

spider

INSECTS

beetle

MYRIAPODS

centipede

CARNIVORES

lion

SEA MAMMALS

whale

PRIMATES

orangutan

HERBIVORES
(5 orders)

elephant

PHYLA

ANNELIDS

earthworm

CHORDATES
(animals with a dorsal nerve chord)

ECHINODERMS

starfish

SUBPHYLA

VERTEBRATES
(animals with a backbone)

CLASSES

FISH

fish

BIRDS

owl

MAMMALS

AMPHIBIANS

frog

REPTILES

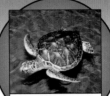

TURTLE

ORDERS

RODENTS

squirrel

INSECTIVORES

mole

MARSUPIALS

koala

SMALL MAMMALS
(several orders)

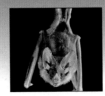

bat

1 Long of Life, Slow of Step

A turtle named Adwaita died in a zoo in Calcutta, India, in March 2006. The death made news around the world because Adwaita, whose name meant "the only one" in the Bengali language of the region, may have been the oldest turtle in the world. According to zoo officials, Adwaita was at least 150 years old, but a few historical records hint that he might have been even older than that. Some people think that Adwaita was the last survivor of four turtles that were gifts to Lord Clive, a British general who fought and lived in India. Clive died in 1774.

Cultures around the world have honored turtles as symbols of long life. And because many turtles walk about in a slow, plodding way, these animals have also come to symbolize slowness, even though some turtles can move quite rapidly, and sea turtles can outswim humans. Turtles also represent strength and survival, which is easy to understand. A turtle lives inside an armored fortress, a sturdy shelter that it carries around with it throughout its life.

THIS ALDABRA TORTOISE, NAMED ADWAITA, WAS AT LEAST A CENTURY AND A HALF OLD WHEN HE DIED IN 2006. BIOLOGISTS CONSIDER ALDABRA TORTOISES ONE OF THE LONGEST-LIVING SPECIES ON EARTH.

The turtle's shell contains a complex creature, a survivor of several hundred million years of evolution, with physical features not found in any other animal. The three hundred or so species of turtles that exist today are adapted for life in a wide range of habitats, from forest ponds to deserts to the open

"Once," the Mock Turtle tearfully says in *Alice's Adventures in Wonderland*, "I was a real Turtle."

ocean. Turtles have long been part of the human world, too. They have served people as food, as pets, and, for thousands of years, as subjects of myths, storytelling, and art.

Turtle, Tortoise, or Terrapin?

Talking about turtles can be a word game, as English mathematician Charles Lutwidge Dodgson recognized in the nineteenth century. Dodgson wrote *Alice's Adventures in Wonderland* (1865) under the pen name Lewis Carroll. In one of the book's scenes, the heroine, Alice, listens as a morose creature called the Mock Turtle, slowly unfolds the tale of his schooldays:

> "When we were still little," the Mock Turtle went on at
> last, more calmly, though still sobbing a little now and
> then, "we went to school in the sea. The master was an
> old Turtle–we used to call him Tortoise–"
> "Why did you call him Tortoise, if he wasn't one?"
> Alice asked.
> "We called him Tortoise because he taught us," said
> the Mock Turtle angrily. "Really you are very dull!"

As Dodgson knew, the terms *turtle* and *tortoise* sometimes refer to different kinds of animals. At other times, however, the two terms seem to be interchangeable. People do not all agree on what the difference is between a turtle and a tortoise, or even on whether there is a difference. To make matters more confusing, people in some parts of the English-speaking world refer to certain turtles with a third term, *terrapin*, which comes from a Native-American language.

People use these terms in a bewildering variety of ways. In North America, for example, some people call any edible turtle a terrapin. Others use that word for just one species of turtle, the

THE DIAMONDBACK TERRAPIN, FOUND ALONG THE ATLANTIC AND GULF COASTS OF NORTH AMERICA, USED TO BE WIDELY HUNTED AS A SOUP INGREDIENT. TODAY IT IS MAKING A COMEBACK IN SOME PROTECTED AREAS.

diamondback terrapin, whose scientific name is *Malaclemys terrapin*. In Great Britain and South Africa, however, any freshwater turtle may be called a terrapin. Some people in those countries use the word turtle for sea-dwelling species only. As for *tortoise*, some apply the term to any turtle that spends even part of its time on land, or that does not live in salt water. Others use it only for "true tortoises," members of one family of turtles that are completely terrestrial, which means that they spend their entire lives on land.

Terrapins and tortoises are also turtles, but to cut through the confusion, some scientists simply call them all chelonians. This is the scientific name for turtles, and it comes from the Greek word *chelone*, which is usually translated as "tortoise" but can also mean "turtle"—as if the subject needed further complication. In this book, *turtle* and *chelonian* may refer to any turtle, but *tortoise* will refer to the true terrestrial tortoises alone. Adwaita, the long-lived turtle who died in the zoo in Calcutta, was a tortoise. He belonged to a species called the Aldabra tortoise, which is found only on a few small islands in the Indian Ocean.

Turtles in Literature and Legend

Although many turtles spend at least part of their lives in water and are swift swimmers, tortoises never swim. Tortoises have thick, heavy shells and big, sturdy legs. They are strong, but they walk very slowly. That is why, in stories from around the world, tortoises prove the point that it is not always the fastest runner who wins the race.

The story of the tortoise and the hare, in the collection of ancient Greek tales known as *Aesop's Fables*, pits a tortoise in a race against a hare. (Hares are close relatives of rabbits, and, like rabbits, they run very fast). The hare, which has boasted about its great speed, is so sure of winning the race that it lies down on the course to take a nap while the tortoise plods along slowly. By the time the hare wakes up, the tortoise has almost reached the finish line. Even with a burst of speed, the hare has no chance of overtaking it.

For centuries people have used Aesop's fable to teach useful moral lessons: Don't boast. Don't loaf. Steady hard work wins out over flashy showing off. Yet a similar story from Africa takes a different turn. In the African fable, the tortoise races against an eagle. This time it wins not by legwork but by using its brain.

The African story tells of a tortoise and an eagle who wanted to marry the same girl. Her father decided that she would marry whichever of the two was first to bring him some salt from the distant seacoast. The tortoise objected that a race would favor the eagle, who could fly much faster than the turtle could walk. Eventually the tortoise agreed to the contest, but only after it was decided that the race would take place in ten months' time.

The tortoise made good use of that ten months. In secret it traveled to the coast, a five month's journey. Along the way it asked other tortoises to help it when the day of the race came. Their job would be to stand at certain points along the route so that the eagle could see them. When the tortoise finally reached the coast, it gathered some salt and then made its slow way back to the starting point. It returned after an absence of ten months—just in time for the race to begin.

As the eagle flew toward the coast, it looked down every so often. To its amazement, it saw that the tortoise appeared to be keeping up with it. When the bird reached the coast, the tortoise was there, gathering salt. Quickly the eagle got some salt and leaped into the air, determined to beat the tortoise back to the starting point. The original tortoise, however, had been hiding near the girl's father all along, with its salt ready. All of the tortoises that the eagle had seen during the race were simply its rival's stunt doubles, posted along the way to make the eagle believe that the tortoise was taking part in the race.

As the eagle approached the end of the race, flying with all its speed, the tortoise stepped out of hiding and carried the salt to the girl's father, just a few steps away. The tortoise won the contest—and the girl—by what some would call cleverness (and others might call cheating). The eagle was so furious about the tortoise's trick that the tortoise decided to live in the water from then on, so that the eagle could not catch and kill it. As the African people who told this tale knew very well, the eagle was a genuine threat to the tortoise. Eagles and other large birds of prey have been observed snatching tortoises from the ground, carrying them into the air, and then dropping them to crack open their shells.

IN AN ANCIENT HINDU VIEW OF THE UNIVERSE, THE WORLD IS SUPPORTED BY ELEPHANTS STANDING ON THE BACK OF A GIANT TURTLE. MANY MYTHS FEATURE TURTLES AS SYMBOLS OF CREATION AND STRENGTH.

Turtles have played a role in the creation myths of some Asian cultures. These myths say that the world is supported on the back of a giant turtle, or that the world was created by a turtle whose body became the land, floating in a vast ocean. Turtles are honored as sacred guests in some Hindu, Buddhist, and Islamic shrines, or temples, in Asia. A colony of black soft-shell turtles, of the species *Aspideretes nigricans*, has been living in an enclosed pond on the grounds of an Islamic shrine near Chittagong, Bangladesh, since at least 1875. The four hundred or so turtles now residing in the tank were once believed to be the last black softshells in existence, but recently a small wild population was found living in the Brahmaputra River.

In ancient China, turtles represented wisdom. People thought that the future could be read in the markings on turtle shells. Images of turtles entwined with snakes were believed to keep evil and danger away; some emperors surrounded themselves with banners bearing that design. The Chinese and Japanese people also regarded turtles as emblems of contentment and long life. They liked to have a tortoise or two living in their gardens, and tortoises or turtles often appear in artworks. Gifts in the form of small turtles made of jade, wood, metal, or pottery were popular, especially at weddings, where they represented a wish for the couple to have a long, happy life together.

The Secret of Long Life?

Adwaita was not the only famous tortoise who died in 2006. In June a tortoise named Harriet died in the Australia Zoo. Originally from the Galapagos Islands, Harriet was thought to be 176 years old at the time of her death, making her older than Adwaita, unless Adwaita really did belong to Lord Clive in the eighteenth century. To many herpetologists—scientists who study turtles and other reptiles—these turtles' great age is no surprise. In recent years, scientists have made amazing discoveries about the longevity of turtles.

Scientists have known for some time that turtles, especially large tortoises, live long lives, but researchers have taken only the first steps toward understanding *why* these animals enjoy such longevity. One key to longevity appears to be the way the turtle's organs age—or, rather, the way they don't age. The organs of a turtle, unlike those of most other animals, do not break down or lose efficiency as the turtle gets older. According to herpetologist Christopher J. Raxworthy of the American Museum of Natural History, the liver, lungs, and kidneys of a hundred-year-old turtle are no different from those of a fifteen-year-old turtle.

Researchers are now looking for clues to the turtle's longevity in its genome, the array of DNA that is the unique genetic signature of turtles as a group. Somewhere in that code may be a gene, or a combination of genes, that protects organs and tissues from the wear and tear of age. If so, the humble turtle may hold the key to medical advances that could one day help to prolong human life.

Biological Basics

"The turtle lives 'twixt plated decks," wrote American comic poet Ogden Nash. He was referring to the turtle's most recognizable feature, the first thing most people think of when they are asked to picture a turtle: its shell. Two sheets of hard plates make up the shell, with the turtle's head, limbs, and body sandwiched between them.

A turtle's shell, however, is not simply a box that encloses the animal. It is part of the turtle's skeleton. In chelonians, the shell is an outgrowth of the ribs, so that in a sense turtles wear their rib cages on the outside of their bodies. The shoulder girdle and the pelvic girdle, which are the arrangements of bones and muscles that attach the forelimbs and hind limbs to the body, are completely contained inside the shell. This unique feature has many advantages, but it has also affected other features of the turtle's anatomy, or physical structure.

A HAWK MAY LAND ON A GALAPAGOS TORTOISE, BUT IT HAS NO HOPE OF LIFTING THE GIANT REPTILE. BIRDS OF PREY, HOWEVER, DO LIFT SMALLER TORTOISES INTO THE AIR, THEN DROP THEM TO BREAK THEIR SHELLS.

Why Shells?

The advantage of having a shell seems obvious. The shell is like a suit of armor that the turtle never removes. It protects the turtle from attacks by possible predators. When threatened, a turtle pulls its head, tail, and legs into the shell. Some kinds of turtles even have hinged shells. They can raise or lower parts of their shells like flaps to cover their tucked-in heads and legs. A few species have heads or limbs that are too large to be pulled inside their shells. Even for these turtles, though, the shell provides considerable protection for the body.

The shells of tortoises protect these animals from more than the teeth and claws of predators. Tortoises have extremely thick, sturdy shells that are often dome-shaped. Because many tortoises share the environments of herds of grazing animals, their shells may have evolved to prevent them from being trampled by animals such as bison, zebras, and wildebeests. A hoof will slide off a rounded, dome-shaped shell more easily than off a flat, pancake-shaped shell. At least one chelonian species, the ornate box turtle of North America, likes to eat insects it finds in the dung of bison or cattle. Other tortoises may also forage for food along game trails and amid herds of grazers, protected by their helmetlike shells.

Turtles' shells also shield the animals from some environmental hazards, such as extreme heat and dryness. While skin can dry out easily in such conditions, a shell helps the animal preserve the moisture in its body. A shell may even protect a turtle from fire. Adult tortoises have been known to survive brush fires in places such as Florida, California, and Greece. Shells that are damaged by fire or that suffer other injuries can heal, if the damage is not too severe.

Some turtles use their shells as tools. The male ploughshare tortoise of Madagascar, a large island in the Indian Ocean, has a projection like a hook on the front of the lower part of its shell. The males fight with these hooks, which they use for stabbing each other and for flipping each other over. Males of other turtle species ram or butt each other with their shells when fighting over females.

For some species of turtles, the shell is like a giant vitamin pill, filled with substances that the turtles need. *Chrysemys picta*, the common painted turtle of North America, can live in northern climates. It survives the cold winters by hibernating in a state of suspended animation, motionless and unbreathing beneath the ice of a pond or lake. During this time, the lack of fresh oxygen in the turtle's bloodstream causes a chemical reaction that deposits lactic acid in the animal's tissues. This acid buildup would kill the turtle if not for the calcium, magnesium, and other minerals stored in the shell. These minerals enter the animal's system and combine with the acid, making it harmless.

Life inside a shell has some drawbacks, however. For one thing, the shell may limit the animal's size. Many species have shells that can continue to increase in size for as long as the turtle lives. In other species, however, the various sections of the shell fuse into a single unit when the turtle reaches adulthood, and growth stops.

The shell also imposes certain limits on the turtle's ability to move. Turtles have varying degrees of difficulty, depending on the species, in righting themselves if they happen to end up on their backs. If they happen to fall on their backs in a hole or depression, they might eventually starve or die of exposure. Most turtles can right themselves, but it sometimes takes a lot of effort. The turtles stretch out their necks, brace their heads against the ground, and work their neck and leg muscles. Sometimes they can dig into the ground with their claws, or even bite the ground. This gives them a grip that they can use to pull themselves over. Another possibility is to build up enough momentum by rocking to flip themselves over.

Shells, Scutes, and Skin

A turtle's shell consists of three main parts. The upper shell is the carapace. The lower shell—the turtle's underside—is the plastron. The carapace and the plastron are linked together by the bridges. There is a bridge on each side of the turtle, between the front leg and the rear leg. In many species the bridges are as firm and strong as the carapace and the plastron. They act as braces, giving the shell extra strength. In a few species, though, the carapace and plastron are held together by bands of the tough, rubbery material called cartilage, which makes the shell more flexible.

Each part of the shell has several layers. The top layer consists of plates called scutes. These usually lie next to each other like floor tiles, but in a few species the scutes on the carapace overlap each other like roof shingles. Most turtles have thirty-eight scutes on the carapace and sixteen scutes on the plastron, for a total of fifty-four. These scutes occur in a wide range of sizes, shapes, textures, and colors, making many distinctive patterns among the turtles of the world.

Scutes are part of the turtle's epidermis, or skin. They are made of a protein called keratin. Animal hair and claws, human hair and nails, feathers, reptiles' scales, and other growths such as rhinoceros horn are also made of keratin, which is tough and durable.

THE PLASTRON OF THIS EASTERN MUD TURTLE HAS TWO HINGES. ONCE THE TURTLE HAS TUCKED IN ITS HEAD, LEGS, AND TAIL, IT CAN RAISE THE FRONT AND REAR EDGES OF THE PLASTRON, ENCLOSING ITSELF COMPLETELY.

Beneath the scutes of a turtle's shell is a second layer of plates. These are made of bone. Most turtles have fifty-nine of these shell bones, fifty in the carapace and nine in the plastron. One key feature of the shell's structure is that the scutes and the bony plates do not line up exactly. If the sutures, or joints,

THE MATAMATA'S BUMPY SHELL AND ROUGH SKIN MAKE THE TURTLE HARD TO SPOT WHEN IT LURKS AMONG THE STONES AND LEAVES OF A RIVER BOTTOM. THE MATAMATA CATCHES PREY BY OPENING ITS LARGE MOUTH AND SUCKING IN WATER— THE PREY IS PULLED IN, TOO.

between the scutes were to be directly over the sutures between the bony plates, the turtle's shell would be weak along those lines. Instead, the bony plates are joined together in one pattern, and the scutes are fused in a different pattern. This means that sutures in the bone are covered by solid scutes, while sutures in the scutes are underlain by solid bone. The only places that the bone and scute sutures line up are along hinges, the flexible joints that allow box turtles and a few other varieties of turtles to raise and lower portions of their shells. The structural weakness of these hinges is balanced by the fact that they allow the turtle to close its shell completely.

Not all turtles have scutes. A number of softshell species, as well as the leatherback sea turtle and the pig-nose turtle, have leathery skin in place of scutes over their bony shells. In the leatherback, the world's largest turtle, even the bone plates are gone, replaced by a network of small bones that support the turtle's tough outer covering of cartilage and keratin.

The skin of turtles is covered all over with scales. Depending upon the species, the scales may be small and smooth or large and lumpy. Some turtles also have skin growths that can serve several purposes. The twist-neck turtle of South America has a row of spines along its neck. When the turtle turns its head to the side and draws it under the carapace, the spines protect its neck. The matamata, a river turtle that is also found in South America, has flaps of skin that give its head and neck the appearance of dead leaves or waterlogged wood. The flaps are camouflage, helping the matamata blend into the background of the shallow forest streams where it lies in wait for prey. In addition, the flaps are sense organs. They feel tiny changes in the water currents, allowing the turtle to "read" its environment for clues about the movements of other animals. Many freshwater turtles have barbels, growths of skin that hang beneath their chins. Scientists are not sure what these sensitive barbels do. By sensing movement like the matamata's flaps, they may help the turtles locate prey in muddy water. Another theory is that the barbels play a role in mating, perhaps by releasing chemicals to attract the opposite sex.

Turtles, like other reptiles, periodically shed their skin. They don't slide out of it in a single piece, as snakes do—their shells make that impossible. Instead, turtles shed their skin a little at a time in small patches. Often they scratch themselves with their claws or rub against logs or rocks to remove the dead skin.

Anatomy of a Turtle

A turtle cannot bend the center of its body, because its ribs are fused to its carapace. Its neck, tail, and limbs are mobile, however. Many turtles have short, stubby tails. The Chinese big-headed turtle is unusual in having a flexible tail that is as long as its carapace, up to 7.2 inches (18.5 centimeters). This tail braces and balances the big-headed turtle when it does something that few other chelonians are known to do: climb trees.

Turtles' limb bones are thick—they have to be, to support the weight of the shell. The thickest of all are the limbs of large tortoises. Not only must these strong, columnlike legs support huge, heavy shells, but they must do so on land. Sea turtles have large shells, too, but they are supported by the water. Sea turtles' limbs are very different from those of tortoises, but they are beautifully adapted to a marine life. The toe bones of each foot are enclosed in a single large, flat digit—a flipper that is highly efficient for swimming. The forelimbs of sea turtles are especially powerful. As the front flippers sweep up and down in a motion similar to the movement of a bird's wings, they propel the turtle through the water. The pig-nosed softshell turtle,

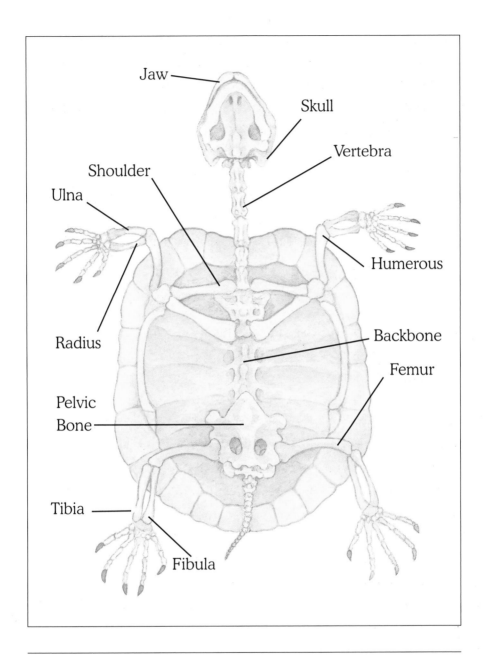

Jaw

Skull

Vertebra

Shoulder

Ulna

Humerous

Radius

Backbone

Femur

Pelvic
Bone

Tibia

Fibula

THE BONY PLATES OF A TURTLE'S SHELL ARE ATTACHED TO THE ANIMAL'S RIBS.
TURTLES ARE THE ONLY ANIMALS WHOSE PECTORAL AND PELVIC GIRDLES—THE
BONES AND MUSCLES THAT ATTACH THEIR LIMBS TO THEIR BODIES—ARE LOCATED
INSIDE THEIR RIB CAGES.

THE ALLIGATOR SNAPPING TURTLE DOESN'T NEED TEETH TO DELIVER A POWERFUL BITE
TO THE FISH THAT ARE ATTRACTED TO THE TURTLE'S WORM-SHAPED TONGUE. WITH
AN AVERAGE ADULT WEIGHT IN THE WILD OF 175 POUNDS (79.5 KILOGRAMS), THESE
TURTLES ARE STRONG AND AGGRESSIVE.

found in southern New Guinea and northern Australia, is the
only freshwater turtle that has also evolved flippers and a wing-
like swimming stroke like that of the sea turtles.

Other freshwater turtles have separate toes and claws,
although most have webs of skin between the claws to add
power to their swimming strokes. Instead of swimming with a
birdlike, flying stroke, freshwater turtles move through the water
by thrusting their hind limbs outward, first one and then the
other, while making paddling motions with their front limbs.

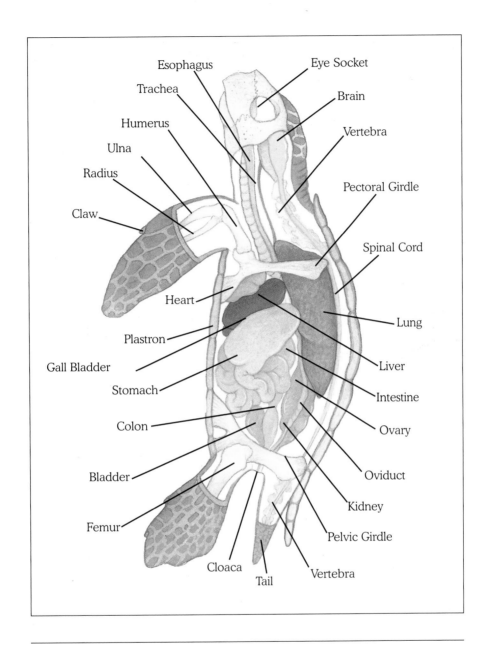

Esophagus
Trachea
Humerus
Ulna
Radius
Claw
Heart
Plastron
Gall Bladder
Stomach
Colon
Bladder
Femur
Cloaca
Tail

Eye Socket
Brain
Vertebra
Pectoral Girdle
Spinal Cord
Lung
Liver
Intestine
Ovary
Oviduct
Kidney
Pelvic Girdle
Vertebra

THE ANATOMY OF A FEMALE SEA TURTLE REVEALS MANY OF THE SAME ORGANS AND
SKELETAL STRUCTURES FOUND IN OTHER ANIMALS WITH BACKBONES. TURTLES HAVE
HEARTS WITH THREE CHAMBERS (COMPARED WITH FOUR CHAMBERS IN HUMANS AND
MANY OTHER MAMMALS) AND BLADDERS THAT CAN STORE WATER FOR WEEKS
AT A TIME.

LEWIS CARROLL GOT THE IDEA FOR HIS SOBBING MOCK TURTLE FROM THE "CRYING" OF SEA TURTLES, WHICH GET RID OF EXCESS SALT THROUGH THEIR TEAR GLANDS.

Freshwater turtles may appear less graceful than sea turtles in the water, but they are much better equipped to walk on land. When sea turtles come ashore to lay their eggs, they have to drag themselves along with their flippers, moving slowly and awkwardly because they are out of their element.

Turtles have no teeth. Most species have hard, sharp-edged jaws that cut or tear their food, whether they eat animals (including other turtles) or plants (including tough varieties such as cacti). Even without teeth, the powerful jaws of a large turtle or tortoise can deliver quite a bite. The alligator snapping turtle of the southeastern United States, for example, can easily snip off the finger of an adult human. Some turtles, such as the green sea turtle, have serrated jaws with sharp little projections like the cutting edge of a saw blade. Softshell turtles are the only chelonians that have soft, fleshy lips instead of hard-edged, beaklike jaws.

All turtles have tongues, which they use for directing food down their gullets. The alligator snapping turtle has a second use for its tongue—as a lure. A fleshy, pink growth on the end of the tongue looks like a small worm. The turtle lies in wait with its mouth open. When a fish moves in to seize the "worm," it is the turtle that does the seizing, snapping down on the luckless fish.

THE DESERT TORTOISE OF THE AMERICAN SOUTHWEST IS WELL ADAPTED TO LIFE IN A CHALLENGING CLIMATE.

A turtle's internal organs are similar to those of most other vertebrates, or animals with backbones. The animal's digestive system has two main parts, the stomach and the intestines. The intestines of plant-eating turtles are considerably longer than the intestines of turtles that eat meat, because it takes longer to break down plant material into nourishment than it does to digest animal protein. Big tortoises that eat large quantities of leaves have intestines that, if laid out straight, would be seven times as long as their shells.

The digestive system ends in a chamber called the cloaca. Solid waste from the intestines passes through the cloaca and out an opening called the anal vent, which is partway down the tail. Urine from the kidneys also leaves the body by this route, and so do the eggs of female turtles. The sex organ of the male turtle is located in the cloaca. During mating, it emerges through the vent.

Like all living things, turtles need water. Because they live in environments that range from the ocean to the desert, they have a variety of ways to get, use, and store water. Sea turtles have no shortage of water—they swim in it. Too much salt in their systems, however, is fatal, just as it is to humans and other animals. When sea turtles eat underwater, salt water enters their gullets along with the food. A valve in their gullets forces the water back out, while the food is kept in by downward-pointing growths of keratin that line the gullet. Sea turtles also have special tear glands that remove salt from the sea water that enters their systems. This excess salt leaves the body in the form of a thick fluid that is as least twice as salty as sea water. When a sea turtle rids itself of salt this way, it appears to be shedding large, shiny tears.

In most animals, the bladder is the organ that holds liquid waste until it is released in the form of urine. A turtle's bladder serves that function, but turtles also use their bladders as canteens, drawing fluid from the bladder back into the bloodstream if they run low on water. A turtle can live on its stored water for an extended period—a month or even more in some species—without taking a drink. Yet when terrestrial turtles have the chance to drink fresh water, they can absorb large quantities of it. Researchers who studied *Gopherus agassizii*, the desert tortoise, which lives in the American Southwest and northwestern Mexico, found that it could drink an amount of water equal to 40 percent of its body weight in less than an hour. During rain showers, these tortoises have been seen digging small basins in the sand to catch and hold the water. When water is scarce or nonexistent, the desert tortoise and its relative the gopher tortoise dig burrows and remain underground. In the dark, cool burrows their bodies use up less moisture than if they remained under the hot sun.

Other tortoises have their own water-conserving tricks. The South African tent tortoise, *Psammobates tentorius*, is one of several species that use their carapaces to channel dew or rainwater into their mouths. The tortoises straighten their hind legs and bend their front legs. This raises the back ends of their shells and lowers the front ends. Water on the carapaces flows downward toward the animals' heads. Gullies or channels in the scutes direct the water into the corners of the turtles' mouths.

Breathing poses special challenges to a creature with a hard shell. Most animals' lungs are enclosed by their ribs. As air flows into and out of the lungs, the ribs move slightly. A turtle's lungs are enclosed within its ribs, but the ribs cannot move—they are fused to the inside of the carapace. The lungs lie just under the carapace, on top of the other internal organs. Sheets of tissue attach the lungs to both the carapace and the other organs. When the organs move downward, the lungs are pulled open, drawing in air. When the organs move upward, the lungs are squeezed, and air is forced out. The organs are moved up and down by the action of muscles inside the turtle's body or by the pumping movement of the turtle's legs as it walks on land or floats on the water's surface.

Turtles that spend time underwater have evolved various ways of getting oxygen. Softshell turtles, matamatas, and some others possess long, tube-shaped nostrils. Like snorkels, the nostrils stick up above the surface of the water, letting the turtle breathe while remaining submerged. Sea turtles have a different strategy. They can hold large volumes of air in their lungs during their dives, and their blood and muscles contain high percentages of chemicals that store oxygen.

Many freshwater turtles can breathe through their skins, a process called cutaneous respiration. Oxygen from the water is absorbed into the bloodstream through the skin, while carbon dioxide, the waste product of breathing, is released into the water. Although no known turtle can live indefinitely on cutaneous respiration alone, every turtle that scientists have studied can obtain some oxygen this way, and many can remain underwater for long periods, especially if they are inactive. In some species, the throat or cloaca is lined with thin tissues that function like a fish's gills. The tissues are packed with many small blood vessels, increasing the surface area of skin that is available to absorb oxygen from the water. Australia's Fitzroy River turtle, which has large gills extending from its cloaca, rarely comes to the surface to gulp air.

Metabolic Magic

Turtles are ectothermic, or cold-blooded, like all reptiles. This means that they do not produce and regulate their own body heat the way humans and other mammals do. Instead, the internal temperature of a turtle's body depends on environmental conditions around it.

Suwannee cooters bask on a log in a Florida river. Basking is a turtle's main tool for absorbing heat from the environment, as cold-blooded creatures must do.

Ectothermy has advantages and disadvantages in terms of metabolism, which is an organism's use of energy. Cold-bloodedness is metabolically inexpensive. It takes much less energy to maintain an ectothermic body than to fuel the heat-producing body of an endothermic, or warm-blooded, creature. Scientists estimate that, on average, reptiles need to take in only about one-thirtieth as much food energy as mammals of the same size.

Another advantage for ectotherms is that, unlike warm-blooded animals, they do not have to maintain the same body temperature and the same level of metabolic activity all the time. They can slow down their metabolism and reduce their activity level to save energy when food is scarce or unavailable, or when environmental conditions are unfavorable. In this

A LEATHERBACK TURTLE RETURNS TO THE SEA AFTER LAYING HER EGGS.

state of reduced metabolic activity, some turtles can go without food for weeks or even months.

The main disadvantage of ectothermy is that cold-blooded animals are, to a great extent, at the mercy of their environments. Because they do not manufacture their own internal heat, they must absorb it from the air, water, or earth around them. This is why most reptiles live in the warmer regions of the planet, and none are found at the poles.

A turtle's ideal temperature depends on its species. Gopher tortoises, which live in warm deserts, function well at an average temperature of about 88° Fahrenheit (31° Centigrade). If a gopher tortoise's temperature drops below 59° F (15° C), the turtle becomes inactive. The pond-dwelling slider turtle, in contrast, has an ideal temperature of around 77° F (25° C) and slows down when its temperature falls below 50°F (10° C). *Chelydra serpentina*, the common snapping turtle, often shares a habitat with the slider but has a slightly different metabolism, remaining active at temperatures as low as 43° (6° C).

Whatever a turtle's ideal temperature, it must remain within a comfortable range of that temperature to survive. Turtles achieve thermoregulation—meaning that they control their body temperature—in a number of ways.

The turtle's shell aids in thermoregulation by acting as an insulator. The shell conserves warmth because heat does not escape through it the way it does through skin. The turtle's main thermoregulatory activity is basking, which is how it gets heat into its system. A turtle finds a warm or sunny spot and stretches out its neck and legs, exposing skin to the warmth. Aquatic turtles may bask while floating on the surface, or they may crawl out of the water onto logs and rocks. Tortoises and other turtles that bask on land seek out rock surfaces or patches of light-colored sand that have been warmed by the sun.

Sea turtles bask by floating at the surface, and they have developed their own forms of thermoregulation to keep them warm during dives into deeper, colder water. A heat exchange takes place in their circulatory systems. Arteries, the blood vessels that carry blood away from the heart to the other parts of the body, lie right next to veins, which carry blood back to the heart. The blood in the arteries has absorbed heat from the muscular action of the heart and from the heat stored in the tissues of the body's core, so it is warmer than the blood in the veins. As blood flows through the thin, exposed flippers, however, it loses heat to the surrounding water. On its way back toward the heart, this cooled blood passes next to the arteries, and heat is transferred to it from the arterial blood. This countercurrent exchange system, as it is called, keeps the turtle's blood from cooling off too fast and slows the rate at which the turtle's body temperature drops. Because of this arrangement, the internal temperature of a diving sea turtle may be as much as 5° F (3°C) warmer than the surrounding water.

Leatherback sea turtles are the chelonian champions of thermoregulation. Although leatherbacks are found throughout the warm waters of the world, they also range farther north and south, into colder waters, than other sea turtles. For example, they have been found in the waters off Greenland, northern Scandinavia, and the Aleutian Islands.

Several factors help leatherbacks survive in cold regions. For one thing, leatherbacks are the largest sea turtles, often weighing more than 1,200 pounds (550 kilograms). When it comes to conserving heat, size is an advantage. Larger animals have less surface area relative to their overall volume than smaller animals have. The bigger the animal, the more body mass it has to hold heat, and the less skin it has, proportional to that mass, to lose the heat.

Leatherbacks generate much of their body heat through muscular activity while they are swimming, but they also have dark skin that absorbs as much heat as possible when they are exposed to sunlight at the surface. The skin is thick and filled with oils, with a layer of fatty tissue just beneath it. These features, not found in other turtles, act as insulation. Leatherbacks also have highly efficient countercurrent exchange systems. With all of these factors acting together, a leatherback swimming in water that has a temperature of 46° F (8° C) may be able to maintain a body temperature of 77° F (25° C).

Thermoregulation is not just for warming up. Turtles also need to cool down at times, because too much heat is as fatal as too little. The easiest way to cool down is simply to move from the surface into deeper water, or from sunlight into shade.

Aquatic species are usually able to maintain their desired temperatures simply by entering the water. Tortoises often cool off by retreating to burrows, but they sometimes use water, too, for the cooling effect that takes place when liquid dries on the skin. If a pond or mud wallow is available, tortoises get wet and then let the moisture evaporate. If no water is available, a tortoise may drool saliva to cool its neck and urinate on its hind legs and tail to lower the temperature of those limbs. Some species also shed tears that cool the face and neck as they evaporate.

Prolonged periods of heat, drought, or cold trigger more extreme survival tactics. A turtle can slow down its metabolism dramatically—in some cases, metabolic activity is so greatly reduced that the turtle enters a state much like death. Withdrawal into an inactive state to escape high temperatures is called estivation. Many turtles and tortoises estivate for a few weeks during the hottest or driest part of the summer. Tortoises usually estivate in a burrow or under logs or rocks. Aquatic turtles, such as the common African helmeted turtle and its river- and pond-dwelling relatives, estivate in holes in the muddy bottoms, sometimes for months at a time. An estivating turtle neither moves nor eats, and its heartbeat and breathing drop from twenty or thirty times a minute to once a minute or less.

Hibernation is similar to estivation, except that hibernation is an escape from the cold. In ponds, under logs or leaf litter, or in burrows, tortoises and turtles wait out the winter in a state of deep inactivity. Unlike bears, which often move about and even wake during their winter hibernations, turtles are completely motionless until warmer temperatures revive them. And while a bear fuels its metabolism with stored fat during the months it spends sleeping, and wakes thin and hungry in the spring, a hibernating turtle uses almost no energy, and weighs almost as much at the end of its hibernation as it did at the beginning.

THE STINKPOT, A NORTH AMERICAN MUSK TURTLE, SPENDS MOST OF ITS TIME IN
PONDS, DITCHES, OR QUIET STREAMS, BUT IT MAY CLIMB ONTO LOW TREE BRANCHES
TO BASK IN THE SUN. THE STINKPOT'S SMALL PLASTRON MAKES THE TURTLE MORE
FLEXIBLE AND MOBILE THEN MANY OTHER SPECIES.

Some species of freshwater turtles in North America can even
hibernate through freezing temperatures. They have evolved a
chemical that acts as a natural antifreeze. Although the turtles'
tissues become frozen, ice crystals do not form in the cells.
When the weather warms up, the tissues are undamaged.

As a way of surviving life's challenges, inactivity has worked
well for chelonians. Some of them even spend more time estivating or hibernating than they spend actively moving about. In

the 1990s scientists made their first close study of Horsfield's tortoise, a species that lives in dry steppes and deserts across central Asia from Iran to western China. In much of the tortoise's range, summers are hot and winters are extremely cold. Researchers who observed Horsfield's tortoise in Kazakhstan found that the animal digs unusually long, deep burrows and spends most of the year secluded in them. It emerges from its burrow in March, after which it eats as much as possible and tries to find a mate. Once the female has laid her eggs, the tortoise again goes underground, in late May or early June. Depending upon summer conditions, Horsfield's tortoise may spend much of the season in its burrow, estivating. It then sinks into a deeper state of hibernation for the winter months. In all, the Horsfield's tortoise is active for five months of the year at most, and often for considerably less than that.

A Turtle's View of the World

Turtles have good eyesight at close range. Scientists do not know how well turtles see things at a distance, but they believe that freshwater turtles can see farther than tortoises. They also think that turtles, like other reptiles, tend to notice motion rather than the shapes of things. Turtles have color vision and are especially sensitive to red, orange, and yellow.

Olfaction, or the sense of smell, is highly developed in turtles, who rely on it to find mates. Both male and female turtles release hormones into the air or water to signal that they are ready to breed. Other turtles pick up these chemical clues with a cluster of special sensory tissues called Jacobsen's organ, located in the roof of the mouth. Turtles also seem able to smell food sources, such as carrion (rotting flesh), garbage, and flowering plants. Some turtles use scent as a defensive mechanism. When threatened, they discharge unpleasant-smelling fluids from glands on their skin, which can make a predator lose interest. One group of chelonians is called musk turtles because of their habit of producing strong smells. The most pungent—at least to human noses—comes from the small North American musk turtle *Kinosternon odoratum*, better known as the stinkpot.

Most turtles are silent, but some species do make sounds, at least occasionally. Tortoises are perhaps the noisiest turtles. They hiss from time to time, and male tortoises utter various sounds —described as barking, coughing, or booming—while mating.

A LEOPARD TORTOISE, NATIVE TO THE SAVANNAS OF AFRICA, FEASTS ON DAISIES.

Scientists do not think, however, that turtles use sound to communicate with each other.

A turtle's ear is covered by a membrane called a tympanum. Often this can be seen as a patch of smooth skin on the side of the turtle's neck, behind the eye. Turtles hear low notes better than high ones. They are also highly sensitive to vibrations that travel though the ground or water, which is why it is hard to sneak up on them. According to folklore in some parts of the world, tortoises "foresee" earthquakes. Geologists are investigating the possibility that turtles may sense subtle earth tremors and, through agitation or unusual behavior, perhaps give warning that an earthquake is coming.

Turtles find their way in the world by using senses and abilities that scientists do not yet fully understand. The best-known navigators among the chelonians are the sea turtles. Each year they make long sea voyages, and each voyage ends at the same small stretch of beach where that turtle breeds. Scientists think that one thing that helps sea turtles find their way back to these spots across immense distances is built-in compasses. Turtles' brains contain extremely tiny pieces of magnetite, a mineral that aligns itself with the earth's magnetic field. Sea turtles also rely on signals from their environment to help them navigate. Such cues may include water currents, the position of the sun and moon, and variations in the salt level of the water.

Tortoises do not make heroic journeys like those of the sea turtles, but the land-dwelling turtles have been known to return to their home territories after being relocated. One leopard tortoise captured in Africa's Serengeti National Park was released 5 miles (8 kilometers) away. For about three and a half months, the tortoise did nothing. Then, after the rainy season started, the tortoise began the long walk home. Two months later, it was back in the area from which it had been removed.

3 Reptile Origins

Turtles have been around for almost a quarter of a billion years. In that long span of time, they have taken strange and wonderful forms. There have been turtles armed with teeth and spikes, sea turtles as big as cars, and lumbering tortoises whose heads were crowned with horns. These and many other turtles are now extinct, but their descendants remain—fourteen families of living turtles that carry on the ancient chelonian lineage.

Mysterious Beginnings

Where did turtles come from? That question is a subject of much debate among paleontologists, the scientists who study ancient life forms. Zoologist and wildlife conservationist Richard Orenstein, author of *Turtles, Tortoises, and Terrapins: Survivors in*

ECHMATEMYS WAS A TURTLE OF THE EOCENE EPOCH, BETWEEN 55 AND 34 MILLION YEARS AGO. FOSSILS HAVE HELPED SCIENTISTS PIECE TOGETHER PART OF THE LONG HISTORY OF CHELONIANS, BUT MAJOR MYSTERIES REMAIN.

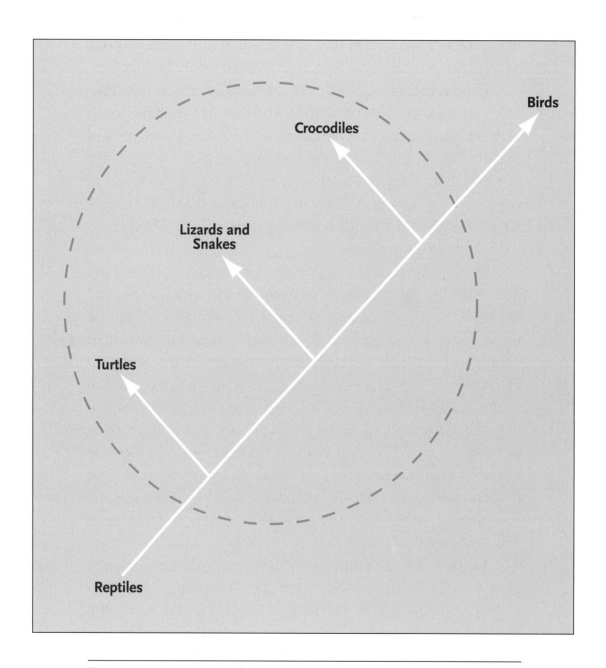

TURTLES ARE THE OLDEST SURVIVING BRANCH OF THE REPTILE FAMILY TREE. THE
DOTTED LINE ENCLOSES THE GROUPS TRADITIONALLY CONSIDERED REPTILES. BECAUSE
OF THEIR EVOLUTIONARY LINK TO THESE GROUPS, BIRDS ARE NOW CLASSIFIED WITH
THE REPTILES BY MANY SCIENTISTS.

Armor (2001) has written that "the origin of turtles remains one of the great unanswered questions of evolutionary biology."

The problem is a shortage of fossils. Scientists can examine fossils of the oldest known turtles, and they can examine fossils of many early kinds of reptiles, but they have not found fossils of the animals that connected those early reptiles with the first turtles. Transitional fossils—that is, fossils showing the stages of evolution between early life forms and those that came later—have been found for many other groups of animals, such as birds, but not yet for turtles.

Many experts believe that transitional fossils for turtles are most likely to be found in the Southern Hemisphere. Several kinds of ancient reptiles that are considered likely candidates for turtle ancestors evolved in Gondwana, a huge landmass that later broke up into the separate continents of the Southern Hemisphere. The most ancient families of living turtles are still found in Africa, South America, and Australia, continents that were once part of Gondwana. Perhaps paleontologists working in those regions will soon unearth transitional fossils that will answer some of their questions about the origin of turtles. Or perhaps not—one of the biggest parts of Gondwana became the continent of Antarctica. It is covered by ice, at least for now, which makes it difficult to search for fossils there.

Turtles, like all modern reptiles, evolved from ancient ancestors that became extinct long ago. Turtles split off to form a distinct group before the modern lizards or other surviving groups of reptiles appeared. But without definite transitional fossils, paleontologists can only speculate about which of the known ancient reptiles might have been the ancestor of turtles.

At one time, experts thought that turtles evolved from *Eunotosaurus*, a small reptile that lived more than 250 million years ago in what is now South Africa. *Eunotosaurus* had broad, flat ribs, and it was possible to picture these ribs evolving into shell plates. Closer study of *Eunotosaurus* fossils, however, showed that its ribs were not at all like those of turtles, which have remained narrow while fusing with the bony plates of the shell. Few scientists now consider *Eunotosaurus* to be a possible ancestor of turtles.

Many paleontologists think that turtles began to evolve during the Permian period, which lasted from about 286 to 245 million years ago. The ancestors of the turtles could have come from one of three groups of ancient reptiles: the procolophonids, the pareiasaurs, or the placodonts.

Procolophonids were large, lizardlike creatures that flourished from 260 to 210 million years ago. One procolophonid, *Owenetta*, had a skull with many features that are found in modern turtles' skulls. The pareiasaurs lived between 260 and 250 million years ago. Some of them also had turtle-like features, including stocky bodies, short thick legs, and armor plating made of scutes. Two pareiasaurs, the 10-foot-long (3-meter-long) *Bradysaurus* and the much smaller *Anthodon*, have been suggested as possible turtle ancestors. The placodonts were marine reptiles. One group of placodonts, called cyamodontoids, had shells with carapaces and plastrons, and they looked a lot like flat sea turtles. A cyamodontoid known as *Henodus* even had its shoulder girdle inside its rib cage, as turtles do. The majority of paleontologists think, though, that *Henodus* and the other cyamodontoids developed separately from turtles, even though both groups had similar features. Biologists call this phenomenon convergent evolution. It explains why, for example, birds and bats both have wings, even though the two groups evolved completely independently.

mlm 362 no number

THE FOSSIL SKULL OF *PROGANOCHELYS*, THE OLDEST KNOWN TURTLE, LOOKS A LOT LIKE THE SKULLS OF MODERN TURTLES. BY THE TIME *PROGANOCHELYS* APPEARED, TURTLES HAD ALREADY LOST THEIR TEETH AND GAINED THEIR SHELLS.

Fossil Finds

The origin of the first turtles remains a scientific mystery, but the development of turtles *after* they evolved is much clearer, thanks to many fossil discoveries. The oldest known turtle is *Proganochelys*. Its fossils were first unearthed in Germany in the 1880s. Since that time, *Proganochelys* fossils have been found in other parts of the world, including Greenland and Thailand.

Proganochelys lived during the Triassic period, some 225 million years ago. Its carapace measured about 2 feet (30 centimeters) long. Scientists think that *Proganochelys* was an aquatic turtle, possibly something like a modern snapping turtle. It may have spent a lot of its time walking along streambeds or swamp bottoms, occasionally coming onto dry land. *Proganochelys* could not retract its head into its shell, and unlike modern turtles it was equipped with toothlike projections called denticles, which grew out of the roof of its mouth. Its neck and tail were covered with thick, stiff scales that formed hard spikes; the scutes of its carapace rose into spiky peaks as well. All in all, *Proganochelys* was a well-armored creature.

Another early turtle from about the same period, *Proterochersis*, was smaller than *Proganochelys*. Scientists consider some of the features of its shell and skeleton more advanced, or closer to those of modern turtles, than those of *Proganochelys*. Because the two turtles lived at around the same time, *Proganochelys* cannot be the ancestor of *Proterochersis*. Both of them must have evolved from an unknown ancestor that lived before either of them.

By 210 million years ago, turtles had evolved into the forerunners of two distinct groups, the pleurodires and the cryptodires, or side-necks and hidden-necks. All living turtles today belong to one of these groups, based on how they retract their heads, or tuck them under their shells. Pleurodires, or side-necks, bend their necks sharply to one side in order to tuck their heads under the overhanging upper surfaces of their shells. When these turtles have retracted their heads, their noses point to one side. Hidden-neck turtles fold their necks backward in a shape like a standing S. When these turtles' heads are retracted, their necks are completely invisible and their noses point forward. Other differences between pleurodires and cryptodires

FOUND IN PONDS AND SLOW-MOVING STREAMS IN EASTERN AUSTRALIA, THIS SIDE-NECK TURTLE TUCKS ITS NECK—WHICH MAY BE AS LONG AS ITS CARAPACE—SIDEWAYS UNDER ITS OVERHANGING SHELL TO SNEAK UP ON PREY. AT THE LAST SECOND THE NECK DARTS OUT LIKE A SNAKE, AND THE TURTLE SNATCHES THE TADPOLE, WORM, OR INSECT.

are less obvious. The structure of the jaw differs somewhat between the two groups of turtles, and so does the structure of the pelvic bones. Sea turtles, which cannot hide either their limbs or their large heads, are considered cryptodires because they share the other anatomical features of that group.

Ancient marine turtles were numerous during the Cretaceous period, which lasted from 144 to 65 million years ago. The largest of these sea-dwelling chelonians was *Archelon ischyros*, the biggest known sea turtle of all time. Although the carapace of a typical *Archelon* was only about 6.3 feet (1.9 meters) long, the turtle was much larger than that when measured from the tip of its snout to the tip of its tail. One fossil specimen found in the 1970s measures 15 feet (4.5 meters) from snout to tail and 16.5 feet (5.25 meters) between the tips of its outstretched flippers. When alive, it could have weighed as much as 4,500 pounds (2,200 kilograms). *Archelon*, like many ancient turtles on land and in the sea, became extinct without leaving any direct descendants.

The oddest group of the ancient turtles has no descendants now living—although one species from that group did survive until very recent times. The meiolaniids were ancient turtles that evolved during the Eocene epoch, between 55 and 34 million years ago. Fossils of meiolaniid species come from Argentina, from Australia, and from several islands near Australia, including Tasmania and New Caledonia. Amazingly, one species of meiolaniid, *Meiolania platyceps*, lived on Lord Howe Island, a small volcanic island off the Australian coast, until it died out about 120,000 to 100,000 years ago.

The meiolaniids were walking fortresses. These large land turtles not only had heavy shells but also bore horns on their heads. In some species the horns stuck out to the side; in others, the horns pointed back. Meiolaniids' long tails were armored, too. The turtles may have used these heavy appendages as clubs.

Based on shell measurement, the largest turtle that ever lived was *Stupendemys geographicus*, which lived about 8 million years ago. A paleontologist named Roger Conant Wood found the first *Stupendemys* fossils in 1976 in the South American nation of Venezuela. Wood named the ancient turtle for its stupendous size and also for the National Geographic

Society, which had paid for his expedition. The largest *Stupendemys* fossil is a carapace that measures 11 feet (3.3 meters) long and 7 feet (2.1 meters) wide. Undoubtedly this huge turtle would be even more impressive if it could be measured from snout to tail, but only its shell was recovered.

Stupendemys was a side-neck turtle, with a flattened shell and thick leg bones. Scientists think that it was aquatic, spending much of its time in fresh water. Its fossils have turned up throughout the Amazon Basin of South America, where a large member of the same family, the arrau or giant river turtle (*Podocnemis expansa*), still lives. Some researchers think that a number of extremely large turtle species inhabited that part of the world between about 12 and 5 million years ago. If so, a future expedition may unearth fossils of a turtle even more stupendous than *Stupendemys*.

4 Turtles of the World

Over the years, scientists have coined various terms for the scientific category that contains turtles. Today, they usually group the species of living turtles together as the order Chelonia. Many scientists use the term Testudines to refer to a larger category that includes both living *and* extinct species.

The order Chelonia is divided into two suborders, Pleurodira and Cryptodira. Each of these suborders is divided into families. Each family contains one or more subgroups called genera. Each genus (the singular form of genera) contains one or more species. The total number of families, genera, and species, however, varies from one expert to the next.

Expert estimates of the number of living turtle species range from 250 to 330. This wide variation is possible because even

NATIVE TO SOUTHERN AND EASTERN EUROPE, HERMANN'S TORTOISES ARE KEPT AS PETS IN MANY PARTS OF THE WORLD. THEY GRAZE ON PLANTS AND ALSO ROAM AROUND IN SEARCH OF FAVORITE FOODS SUCH AS SNAILS AND FALLEN FRUIT.

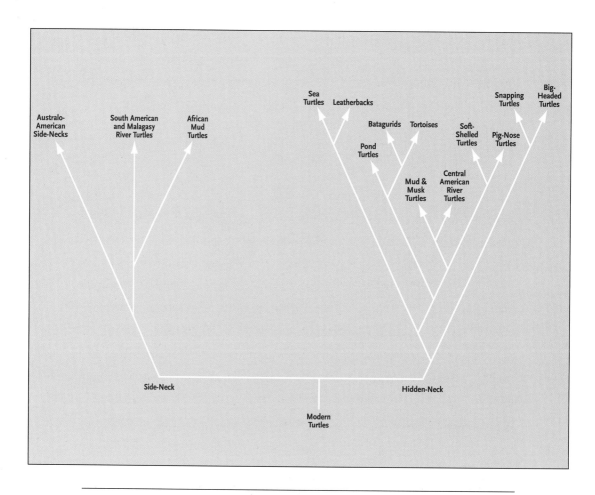

A TURTLE FAMILY TREE SHOWS THAT THE MAIN DIVISION IS BETWEEN SIDE-NECK AND HIDDEN-NECK SPECIES. MANY SCIENTISTS RECOGNIZE THESE FOURTEEN FAMILIES OF MODERN TURTLES. SOME EXPERTS, HOWEVER, CLASSIFY CHELONIANS INTO A DIFFERENT NUMBER OF FAMILIES.

experts do not always agree on whether two animals belong to different species or the same species, or on how to classify a particular turtle. In addition, some herpetologists include species that are known only from one or two specimens, or that have not been seen for many years, while other scientists drop these species from the count. Where genera and families are concerned, scientists follow several different systems of classification. One of the most widely used systems recognizes fourteen families of modern turtles. Three of these families are pleurodires, and eleven are cryptodires.

Side-Neck Turtles

The suborder of pleurodires, or side-necks, contains the oldest groups of living turtles. Pleurodires are found only on the southern continents. There are three pleurodire families, but nowhere do all three occupy the same continent.

African Mud Turtles. The family Pelomedusidae, often called the African mud turtles or terrapins, is the oldest known group of turtles alive today. This family evolved about 120 million years ago. It now lives only in Africa and in the neighboring Indian Ocean islands of Madagascar and the Seychelles group. (One species, *Pelusios niger*, is also found in southern Florida and the West Indies. Humans in recent times brought the turtles to those locations; the turtles then escaped or were released and founded small wild populations.)

African mud turtles are the most widespread group of turtles in Africa south of the Sahara Desert. They live in streams, swamps, lakes, and temporary water holes and rain pools. If necessary, they travel across dry land to move from one body of water to another. Some species have hinged plastrons. After tucking in their heads and forelegs, they can raise the front part of the plastron like a drawbridge, sealing themselves behind a protective barrier of shell.

South American and Malagasy River Turtles. The family Podocnemididae has an unusual geographic distribution. One species in this family, *Erymnochelys madagascariensis*, or the Malagasy big-headed turtle, lives in the slow-moving rivers and

THE ARRAU, OR GIANT SOUTH AMERICAN RIVER TURTLE, IS WELL NAMED—IT IS THE CONTINENT'S BIGGEST TURTLE, ALTHOUGH SOME EXTINCT SPECIES WERE MUCH LARGER.

lowland lakes of western Madagascar, near Africa. All of the other species live in the rivers of the Orinoco and Amazon basins in northern South America.

This family contains the largest living pleurodire, the arrau or giant river turtle of the Amazon. Females of this species are larger than males. They may have carapaces up to 28 inches (70 centimeters) in length and reach weights of 55 pounds (25 kilograms). The arrau has long been highly prized as a food source, for both its meat and its eggs, and turtles were harvested in great numbers, especially when they came ashore to lay their eggs on sandy beaches. By the middle of the twentieth century the species was gravely endangered. The governments of Brazil and Venezuela set aside some nesting beaches as protected areas, and since that time the arrau's numbers have increased, but constant watchfulness is needed to prevent poaching, or illegal hunting. With limits on the hunting of the arrau, people have increased their harvesting of the smaller species of river turtles, some of which are now becoming rare.

As the common snapping turtle pulls in its head, the skin of its neck forms a tubelike collar like that on a turtleneck sweater.

A GREEN TURTLE FEEDS ON ALGAE GROWING ON A CORAL REEF IN MALAYSIA.

Australo-American Side-Neck Turtles. The family Chelidae, a group of freshwater river and forest turtles, is the largest family of side-neck turtles, with 30 or so species in Australia and the nearby island of New Guinea, and another 20 species in South America. Many of the species in this family have very long necks. The matamata belongs to the family Chelidae, as does Spix's snake-necked turtle, which has small spines on its neck and limbs. Several South American species of toad-headed

VOLUNTEERS RELEASE A LOGGERHEAD TURTLE INTO THE SEA IN FLORIDA. SEA TURTLES ARE SOMETIMES CAUGHT AND TAGGED SO THAT SCIENTISTS CAN TRACK THEIR MOVEMENTS.

The shell of the hawksbill, polished into a hard, shiny substance called tortoiseshell, used to be made into combs, jewelry, and other objects.

turtles have wide, flat heads. The Australian members of the family include the dinner-plate tortoise, which has a smooth, almost round carapace, and *Chelodina expansa*, the giant snake-necked turtle, the largest member of the family with a carapace length of about 19 inches (48 centimeters).

A LEATHERBACK HATCHLING WORKS ITS WAY OUT OF THE NEST. ONCE FREE, IT WILL
DASH TO THE SEA.

SPINY SOFTSHELL TURTLES CAN BURY THEMSELVES IN SHALLOW WATER, BREATHING THROUGH LONG NOSTRILS THAT STICK UP ABOVE THE WATER'S SURFACE LIKE SNORKELS.

Hidden-Neck Turtles

The suborder of cryptodires, or hidden-neck turtles, includes the most recently evolved family of chelonians. Cryptodires are more widely distributed than pleurodires. Although many cryptodire families live only on the northern continents, sea turtles are found around the world, and several other families inhabit the Southern Hemisphere.

Snapping Turtles. The family Chelydridae has just two species, the common snapping turtle and the alligator snapping turtle. The common snapping turtle is found from southern Canada to Ecuador in northern South America, but the alligator snapper has a much smaller range in the southeastern United States. While common snapping turtles live in almost any body of water and frequently come out onto land, alligator snappers prefer large rivers and seldom venture out of the water, except to lay eggs.

The Big-Headed Turtle. The family Platysternidae consists of a single species, *Platysternon megacephalon*, the big-headed turtle of southern China and Thailand. This turtle's large head, which is covered with a single hard scale, can be half as wide as its carapace. The big-headed turtle is a stream-dweller that burrows into the bottom by day and comes out to hunt at night.

Sea Turtles. The family Cheloniidae includes all of the sea turtles except the leatherback. There are six species in the family. Four of them—the olive ridley, the green, the loggerhead, and the hawksbill—are found in warm or temperate ocean waters around the world. (Some biologists recognize two distinct species of green sea turtle, the Pacific and the common.) The other two species have more limited ranges. The Kemp's ridley turtle lives only in the Atlantic Ocean and nests on a stretch of beach in Mexico, while the flatback turtle is found only along Australia's northern shores.

Sea turtles are streamlined, powerful swimmers that are so well adapted to life in a marine environment that they rarely come onto land. All sea turtles hatch on land and then hurry into the sea. Males may never again leave the ocean. They can eat, mate, and bask in the water. Females, however, have to crawl up onto beaches to lay their eggs. In addition, both male and female green sea turtles occasionally come onto the shore to bask. Most species of sea turtles are meat-eaters, but adult green sea turtles and young hawksbills feed mostly on sea grass. These turtles sometimes gather in large numbers at the sites of undersea prairies to browse on the vegetation, like herds of grazing cattle.

The Leatherback Sea Turtle. The only species in the family Dermochelyidae is the world's largest turtle, and the one with the greatest geographic range. The leatherback is set apart from other sea turtles by its leathery, shell-less carapace, which has seven ridges running from front to back. These ridges serve the same purpose as the keel of a boat, helping the turtle cut efficiently through the water. Leatherbacks spend time far from land, in the central ocean basins, as well as in the coastal waters of every continent except Antarctica. Their main food is jellyfish, but they eat other foods as well, including shrimps, fish, and even smaller turtles. Leatherbacks can dive deeper in search of prey than any other turtles, down to depths of 3,300 feet (1,000 meters).

Soft-Shelled Turtles. The family Trionychidae contains more than 20 species of soft-shelled turtles. These aquatic turtles, which often spend prolonged periods underwater, are found in North America, Africa, India, and Asia. Their carapaces are covered with leathery skin rather than hard scutes, and they are typically rather round and flat. Soft-shells tend to have long, narrow heads, snorkel-like snouts, and broad, webbed feet. Members of this family have only three toes on each foot; most other turtles have four or five. One of the largest species in the family is *Chitra indica*, the Indian narrow-headed giant softshell, which may

THE PIG-NOSE TURTLE IS ALSO CALLED THE FLY RIVER TURTLE AFTER THE PLACE WHERE IT WAS FIRST SEEN BY EUROPEAN SCIENTISTS—A LARGE WATERWAY IN NEW GUINEA.

reach weights of up to 264 pounds (120 kilograms). Bibron's frog-faced giant softshell, found in the rivers of southern New Guinea, is comparable in size but less common.

The *Pig-Nose Turtle*. The sole species in the family Carettochelyidae is the pig-nose turtle, *Carettochelys insculpta*,

A GIANT MUSK TURTLE USES ITS LARGE MOUTH AND STRONG JAWS TO SEIZE PREY AND ALSO TO DEFEND ITSELF FROM THREATS, INCLUDING OTHER AGGRESSIVE MUSK TURTLES.

which lives in southern New Guinea and a small area in northern Australia. It is the only cryptodire found in Australia, other than the sea turtles. With a flattened shell and flipperlike limbs, the pig-nose turtle resembles the sea turtles. It has been

RHINOCLEMMYS PULCHERRIMA, A WOOD TURTLE FOUND IN MEXICO AND MANY PARTS OF CENTRAL AMERICA, LIVES IN PONDS OR SLOW-MOVING RIVERS, AS DO MOST WOOD TURTLES. THESE AMERICAN BATAGURIDS GOT THEIR NAME BECAUSE THEIR SHELLS HAVE GRAINS AND PATTERNS LIKE THOSE SEEN IN WOOD.

A SPECKLED PADLOPER, THE WORLD'S SMALLEST TORTOISE, CONFRONTS ITS GIANT RELATIVE, THE ALDABRA TORTOISE. IN NATURE, HOWEVER, THE RANGES OF THESE TWO SPECIES DO NOT OVERLAP.

known to leave its rivers and lagoons and enter salt marshes and shallow coastal waters where sea turtles live. The pig-nose turtle appears often in the art of Australia's Aborigines, who have long harvested it for food.

Central American River Turtle. Millions of years ago the family Dermatemydidae was represented by many species throughout the Northern Hemisphere. Today only one species survives: *Dermatemys mawii,* the Central American river turtle.

Found in southern Mexico, Belize, and northern Guatemala, this aquatic, vegetarian turtle is highly endangered by overharvesting for food.

Mud and Musk Turtles. The approximately thirty species of the family Kinosternidae are all found in North, Central, or South America. More than half of all species live in Mexico and northern Central America. Most members of this family are small or medium-sized turtles, brownish or greenish in color, often with yellow stripes on their necks. Mud turtles spend more

THE EXTREMELY RARE PLOUGHSHARE TORTOISE IS JUST ONE OF MANY THREATENED SPECIES UNIQUE TO MADAGASCAR, A LARGE ISLAND OF GREAT BIODIVERSITY OFF THE COAST OF AFRICA.

time on land than musk turtles. The eastern mud turtle of North America may spend most of its time on land and often hibernates in a burrow or a pile of leaves.

The largest member of the family is the northern giant musk turtle, which lives in southern Mexico and western Honduras. Its carapace can measure up to 16 inches (40 centimeters) long. An aggressive hunter with a large head and strong jaws, this turtle preys on other turtles, especially mud turtles that are unlucky enough to cross its path.

Asian and American River Turtles. The Bataguridae are a large family of about sixty-five or seventy species. About eight or

RED-EARED SLIDERS WERE ONCE SOLD BY THE MILLIONS AS CHILDREN'S PETS. AS A RESULT OF INTERNATIONAL TRADE, THESE NORTH AMERICAN POND TURTLES ARE NOW ESTABLISHING THEMSELVES ON OTHER CONTINENTS.

WITH THEIR HIGH, DOMED SHELLS, BOX TURTLES RESEMBLE TORTOISES BUT BELONG TO THE POND TURTLE FAMILY. ALTHOUGH THEY SPEND MOST OF THEIR TIME ON LAND, THEY ARE GOOD SWIMMERS.

nine species, called wood turtles, live in the Americas. Most batagurid species are found in southern Asia, where they are under great stress from overhunting for food markets and for the pet trade.

The number of surviving batagurid species is uncertain because many species have not been seen for years. At the same time, new

Pancake tortoises are good climbers that move faster than other tortoises. When threatened, a pancake tortoise hurries to the nearest hiding place. With a flat, somewhat flexible carapace, the tortoise can wedge itself into a narrow crevice among rocks or tree roots.

Basking on a log, a painted turtle stretches out its neck to expose as much skin as possible to the sun and warm air.

species are occasionally discovered. In 1995, for example, an animal dealer purchased seven turtles on the Indonesian island of Sulawesi. They turned out to be the first recorded specimens of a new species, the Sulawesi forest turtle, *Leucocephalon yuwonoi*.

Some turtles in the batagurid family are entirely or mostly terrestrial. *Melanochelys tricarinata*, the keeled hill turtle of India and Bangladesh, is one example. It lives in hilly forests. A related species shares the forest habitat of rhinoceroses in Nepal; it incubates its eggs by burying them in the sand where rhinos urinate. Other batagurids are aquatic and live in rivers and ponds. Many members of this family have colorful spots and stripes. One of the most striking is the four-eyed turtle, which has four large spots that look like eyes on the back of its head. These probably evolved to startle and confuse predators.

Tortoises. The family Testudinidae has more than fifty species worldwide. Tortoises are found on all continents except Australia and Antarctica. They range in size from the giant tortoises of the Aldabra Islands in the Indian Ocean and the Galapagos Islands in the Pacific to the tiny pygmy tortoises of South Africa. These little tortoises are also called padlopers, which means "trail walkers" in Afrikaans, the language of the first Europeans to settle the area. The smallest of them, the speckled padloper, *Homopus signatus*, weighs about 3 ounces (85 grams) when fully grown. Males of the species may have carapaces only 3 inches (8 centimeters) long. At the other end of the spectrum, Aldabra and Galapagos tortoises have reached weights of 675 pounds (300 kilograms) and carapace lengths of 40 inches (106 centimeters) in the wild. (Captive animals are often larger but are not considered typical of the species).

Herpetologists generally consider Madagascar's ploughshare tortoise to be the rarest member of this family. Another extremely rare species is *Malacochersus tornieri*, the pancake tortoise, found in the East African nations of Kenya and Tanzania. Most tortoises have high, domed shells, but the pancake tortoise—as its name suggests—is flat. Like the padlopers and some other small tortoises, it lives in rock piles and is able to climb about nimbly on the rocks. The pancake tortoise's flat shape lets it creep into narrow cracks or crevices. Once it has done so, it can expand its body to wedge itself in place. It is able to do this because its shell is softer and more flexible than the shell of any other tortoise, with many openings between the bony plates of the inner layer. When the tortoise bulges its body outward, its plastron and carapace also bulge, securing the tortoise in place.

Pond Turtles. The large family Emydidae evolved more recently than any other family of living turtles—about 80 million years ago. The family contains about fifty species in North America, Europe, and the Near East, with three species in South America. The majority of emydid species, about three dozen of them, are found in North America east of the Mississippi River. One species, the painted turtle, is the only chelonian that is found clear across North America. Another, the bog turtle is North America's smallest turtle, measuring only about 4.4 inches (11 centimeters) in length.

Many of the turtles that are most familiar to Americans, Canadians, and Europeans belong to this family. These include the pond turtles, sliders, cooters, painted turtles, wood turtles, and box turtles. Most of the emydids are aquatic, but the box turtles are largely terrestrial.

The most widespread turtle in the world, aside from the various species of sea turtles, is probably a small North American emydid called the red-eared slider. Bred in vast numbers for sale as inexpensive pets during the middle of the twentieth century, red-eared sliders were carried around the world by humans. Wild populations of these turtles now exist in Africa, Europe, Asia, and Australia. Some countries have banned the import of sliders for fear that the newcomers will harm native species of pond turtles. It may be impossible, however, to get rid of the slider populations that people have already introduced into places where they do not occur naturally. These adaptable shelled survivors are making themselves at home in ponds and streams around the world.

5 The Life Cycle

No two turtle species follow exactly the same path through life, but certain features of the chelonian life are universal. All turtles give birth to their young in the form of eggs, for example. Turtles give no parental care to their young and do not have family life, but some species do have social relationships with others of their kind. Herpetologists admit that they know fairly little about many kinds of turtles, and some species have not yet been observed in the wild. Future turtle studies may well disclose a few surprises.

Courtship and Mating

Turtles do not form permanent mating pairs. Some turtles, such as spotted turtles, hibernate in groups, so that when spring arrives and they come out of hibernation, males and females are

GREEN SEA TURTLES SOMETIMES MATE IN THE SURF WHERE THE SEA MEETS THE LAND. THE FEMALE WILL LAY HER EGGS FARTHER INLAND ON THE BEACH. FEMALES OF THIS SPECIES BREED ONCE EVERY THREE TO SIX YEARS.

already in close company and ready to mate. In most species, however, the male seeks out a female partner, possibly competing with other males for the right to mate with her. Male tortoises, slow though they may be, are known for their fierce attacks on rivals and their determined pursuit of females.

Males of a few freshwater species take on special mating colors, bright stripes, or spots on the skin during the breeding season. Otherwise, turtles look pretty much the same year in and year out. Nearly all species engage in some form of courtship behavior before they get down to the business of mating. Depending upon the species, their courtly gestures can include smelling each other's tails, stroking each other's faces and necks with their claws, blowing bubbles, blinking, nodding or head-bobbing, or touching noses. Tortoises often employ rougher tactics, such as butting their prospective partners with their shells or even biting them.

Mating can be hazardous for either the male or the female, again depending upon the species. Among sea turtles and large tortoises, males are larger than females. When the male Galapagos or Aldabra tortoise rests his weight on the female's shell during mating, he may force her down into mud or sand. Female sea turtles have been known to drown during mating if they cannot get their heads above water to breathe. In many other species, however, the females are larger than the males, or the same size. The males still face the challenge of positioning themselves properly behind the females, so that the cloacal vents in their tails are close together. Male tortoises and box turtles, whose mates have high, dome-shaped shells, sometimes have to stand almost upright on their hind legs to achieve mating. They usually clasp the female's shell with their front claws or their teeth, but even so, a male may fall over onto his back.

The act of mating may last anywhere from a minute to an

hour. Some species repeat it, mating two or even three times, before the male and female wander off in their separate directions. At that point the male's work is done. He will never see his mate's eggs or his offspring.

A female's eggs may be fertilized as soon as she has mated, or she may store the male's sperm in her body for weeks or even months. This allows fertilization to take place at the appropriate time for the eggs to hatch during the best seasonal and weather conditions.

Normally, once a female is carrying fertilized eggs, she lays her clutch, or batch of eggs, between forty-five and ninety days later. Many species, however, have the ability to put egg-laying on hold. They can carry their ready-to-lay eggs inside their bodies for months. Like storing the sperm, this egg-carrying adaptation gives female turtles more control over when to lay their eggs, increasing their chances of producing young. Another mechanism for the same purpose is multiple clutches. A female turtle may release her eggs in several batches, spaced out in different locations or at different times. If the weather or some other condition takes a bad turn, she has literally not put all of her eggs in one basket. One or two clutches may fail, but the third could still survive. As for the number of eggs in a clutch, the majority of species lay between seven or eight and twenty-five or thirty eggs. The pancake tortoise lays just one egg, while the hawksbill and other sea turtles produce huge clutches, sometimes numbering more than two hundred eggs.

Nests, Eggs, and Hatchlings

A female turtle has only one responsibility toward her unborn young: to make a nest. Nesting habits are highly varied. Females of some species, such as American wood turtles, simply deposit their eggs among leaves or other vegetation. Others lay them beneath overhanging rocks or next to logs. Most turtles, though, excavate nests for their eggs.

A nest can be as simple as a shallow basin scratched into the sand by the female's hind legs, or as complex as a deep burrow filled with vegetation. Some turtles moisten their nests with water or urine, either to seal the nests or to prevent the eggs from becoming too hot. One turtle, the Suwannee River cooter, digs three nests. One nest holds most of her eggs. It is carefully camouflaged. The other two hold only a few eggs each and are covered carelessly. A raccoon or other predator is likely to focus on the two easy-to-find decoy nests and may miss the main nest.

Turtles must position their nests carefully to keep the eggs from becoming too cold or too hot, or from getting flooded. The temperature at which the eggs incubate in their nest, perhaps covered by a layer of vegetation to increase warmth, determines how long it takes for the embryos to reach the point of hatching. Under warm conditions embryos develop faster.

Nest temperature has another important function, as scientists discovered in the 1960s. For some groups of turtles, it determines the gender of the offspring. This phenomenon, called temperature-dependent sex determination (TSD), is not unique to turtles. It appears in some other reptiles, such as crocodiles. Depending upon the temperature inside the eggs, the young will develop as all males, all females, or a mix of males and females. Some biologists have suggested that the combination of TSD and climate warming could spell disaster for turtles. If the average temperature of a turtle's habitat rises enough to effect all nests, the result could be a population of turtles all of one gender. Not all turtles, however, are subject to TSD. In softshell turtles and some other groups, the gender of the young is determined by sex chromosomes, as it is in humans and other mammals. This system is called genetically based sex determination (GSD).

However their sex is determined, the young turtles must eventually break out of their eggshells—unless they have been devoured by seagulls, raccoons, or any of the other predators that eat turtle eggs. Although some turtles lay hard, brittle eggs like those of birds, most turtle eggs are leathery and slightly flexible. A young turtle needs something sharp to break out. It uses a point or small spike of keratin called an egg tooth, located on the end of its nose. Once the turtle has left the egg, this egg tooth disappears.

Herpetologist Archie Carr, a pioneer of turtle study, once observed a young musk turtle hatching. It took three days for the turtle to poke a hole in the eggshell and work its way out. Escaping from the egg is not the hatchling's only task. It then has to get out of the nest. A single hatchling may be unable to break out of a burrow that has been sealed with dried urine or mud. Sometimes a whole clutch of hatchlings has to work together, pushing with their shells and scrabbling with their claws, to unseal a nest.

By the time the hatchlings emerge, their mother has long since departed. The young turtles are on their own. They do not have to find food immediately, because the yolk sac that nourished them as they developed inside the egg has not completely disappeared. Its remnants are attached to the hatchling's plastron and will be enough to feed it for a day or two at least. But although the hatchling need not worry about food, predators are another story. Newly hatched turtles are notoriously vulnerable—tiny, short-legged, inexperienced. The most hazardous time in a turtle's life is the first few hours, or even minutes, when it must make the transition from the nest to a new stage of life in the sea, in a stream or pond, or on the forest or desert floor. The

LOGGERHEAD HATCHLINGS MAKE THE MOST IMPORTANT RUN OF THEIR LIVES, FROM THE NEST TO THE SEA. ONCE THEY REACH THE WATER, THEY WILL STILL BE VULNERABLE, BUT THE GREATEST DANGER WILL HAVE PASSED.

scurry of hundreds of sea turtle hatchings across a beach, while gulls and other predators dive in to pick them off, is one of the most impressive (and anxiety-producing) sights in nature.

Adult Life

Most hatchlings do not survive the first stages of life. Small, weak, and vulnerable, many of them fall to predators or to disease or exposure. Those who make it are the foundation of a new generation. For most turtles, however, growing up takes time. A turtle may not reach its adult size for several years. It may not reach sexual maturity, the point at which it is ready to breed, for several more years after that.

Large turtles that have long lives, such as giant tortoises and sea turtles, mature quite slowly. Females may not mate until they are twenty-five or even thirty years old. Turtles can, however, continue to produce young for the rest of their lives, even into old age, if they can find mates.

Most turtles' lives are fairly solitary, except at breeding and nesting times. Some freshwater turtles, however, live in small groups that share a habitat, such as a pond, and remain more or less intact for years. The individual turtles do not interact much, but they tolerate each other's presence and frequently bask in groups. The giant Galapagos and Aldabra tortoises are also somewhat social, moving about in groups, sharing mud wallows, and feeding side by side. Long-lived, slow-moving beasts such as these, who have evolved on small islands, have grown used to the presence of their own kind. Perhaps they have even developed a taste for companionship.

6 Chelonian Conservation

Turtles are in terrible trouble. In 2006 the World Conservation Union (IUCN), an international association of conservation groups that monitors the status of wildlife around the world, listed 205 turtle species on its annual Red List of Threatened Species. For 12 species, the IUCN did not have enough information to report on their status. For the rest of the species, the picture was bleak.

More than 50 species, including the Galapagos and Aldabra giant tortoises, were labeled Vulnerable, which means that their populations are small and they are at risk of becoming threatened. Another 50 were categorized as Near Threatened. The arrau of South America was listed as Conservation Dependent, meaning that it is not expected to survive without continued active protection. Forty-five species were listed in the more

A KEMP'S RIDLEY SEA TURTLE STRUGGLES IN A NET. UNABLE TO FREE ITSELF, THE TURTLE WILL DROWN OR STARVE. SUCH ACCIDENTAL DEATHS—AND THERE ARE MILLIONS OF THEM EACH YEAR—ARE CALLED BYCATCH IN THE FISHING INDUSTRY.

serious category Endangered. The most serious category of all, Critically Endangered, had 26 species, including the Central American river turtle, the newly discovered Sulawesi forest turtle, and the Kemp's ridley, hawksbill, and leatherback sea turtles.

How did turtles get into such a precarious position? Although natural predators kill turtles every year, as they have always done, humans are the culprit in the current plight of the turtle. Human activity is taking turtles out of the wild at an alarming rate.

Harvesting Turtles

Olduvai Gorge is a canyon in East Africa where some of the oldest remains of human ancestors have been found. Turtle fossils bearing evidence of ancient damage have also been found at Olduvai. These fossils show that 2 million years ago people had started eating turtles. They have not stopped since.

In almost every part of the inhabited world, people have eaten turtles and tortoises, or their eggs. Large tortoises, slow and easy to catch, were irresistible to the seafarers of earlier centuries, who took enormous numbers of Galapagos, Aldabra, and other now-extinct varieties of giant tortoises aboard their ships. From the point of view of the ships' cooks, the tortoises were ideal provisions. They did not need to be fed, and they could live for months, if necessary, before being killed and eaten. Some species of island tortoises were eaten into extinction in this way.

It is not always the flesh of turtles that is the hunter's quarry. Often it is the turtles' eggs. By raiding nests and removing eggs, people can drastically reduce the entire future population of a species. The arrau is a good example. The native people of Amazonia have eaten this turtle and its eggs for hundreds, probably thousands, of years. In 1541 the Spanish conquistador Francisco de Orellana and his followers became the first Europeans to travel down the length of the Amazon River. Along the way, they noticed that turtles were a primary food in just about every village. In one village they counted more than a thousand turtles in pens, waiting for the cookpot.

As the human population of Amazonia increased, so did the pressure on the arrau. Henry Walter Bates was a naturalist who traveled through the area in the mid-nineteenth century. He saw that people still kept arrau in ponds behind their houses, much as North American farmers might keep a few chickens or pigs. The difference was that the arrau were not bred in captivity—they were taken from the wild, as many as 2 million of them a year from one Brazilian state. Bates realized that the arrau faced a double threat. The turtles were hunted for their meat, and at the same time people were taking their eggs and selling them as a cash crop. He estimated that 48 million eggs were taken each year and wrote, "The universal opinion of the settlers on the Upper Amazon is that the turtle has very greatly decreased in numbers, and is still annually decreasing."

By the 1970s biologists warned that the arrau would become extinct in about ten years if the exploitation of the turtle continued unchanged. Government programs to protect nesting sites and to educate people about turtle conservation helped—the arrau is not yet extinct. But it is critically endangered, and poachers have wiped out some arrau populations even in conservation zones. The arrau will probably not survive in the wild without beefed-up protection.

Other turtles that are being severely overhunted for food include the Central American river turtle, the radiated tortoise of Madagascar, the Nile softshell of Africa, and the pig-nose turtle. Many Asian softshell and river turtles are under extreme

ITS BEAUTIFUL STAR-PATTERNED SHELL HAS MADE MADAGASCAR'S RADIATED TORTOISE A DESIRABLE PIECE OF MERCHANDISE IN THE ILLEGAL PET TRADE. ALSO HUNTED FOR FOOD, THE TORTOISE IS NOW ENDANGERED.

hunting pressure. Tons of wild-caught turtles are being shipped each week from Southeast Asian nations such as Thailand and Indonesia to China, where wild turtles have all but disappeared. There they are used as food and in recipes for folk medicines. The Sulawesi forest turtle is an example of the great destructive power of the Chinese turtle market. For a few years after the species was discovered in 1995, large numbers of Sulawesi forest turtles were seen in Chinese marketplaces. Less than a decade later the species had vanished from those same marketplaces because it had become so scarce.

Food is not the only reason people harvest turtles. The ancient Egyptians prized the scutes of the hawksbill sea turtle, which they captured in the Red Sea. They carved the scutes into ornaments and polished the mottled brown-and-yellow pattern until it gleamed. This substance later came to be known as tortoiseshell, although the hawksbill is not a tortoise.

Like the ivory of an elephant's tusks, tortoiseshell is a beautiful and valuable substance that has threatened the survival of the species that produces it. In 1977, in the face of declining hawksbill populations, the species was listed in Appendix I of the Convention on International Trade in Endangered Species (CITES), which prohibits commerce in the listed species for the 150 or so nations that have signed the CITES agreement. An illegal trade in tortoiseshell and stuffed baby hawksbills continues, however. Some conservationists think that poachers may simply be stockpiling hawksbill scutes, hoping that the trade will become legal once again.

The trade in tortoiseshell has been around for centuries, but a new and even more serious threat to turtles has arisen in the past fifty years or less. The pet trade removes millions of turtles from the wild each year. Many of those turtles belong to endangered, protected, or rare species.

The pancake tortoise illustrates how destructive the uncontrolled trade in live turtles can be, both for individual animals and for an entire species. In the 1980s pancake tortoises started appearing in ever-larger numbers in the pet shops of the United States, Europe, and Japan. Expensive at first, they soon fell in price as traders purchased increasing numbers of them from Africans who collected them in the wild. The 1990s brought several well-publicized cases of airport officials uncovering quantities of pancake tortoises being shipped in brutally cruel conditions. The outrage aroused by these cases led to surveys of pancake tortoise populations in Tanzania. Researchers found that the number of wild tortoises had dropped dramatically since the start of large-scale collection for the pet trade. The government of Tanzania took a strongly pro-turtle step by outlawing the export of pancake tortoises—which also made it illegal for any countries in the CITES agreement to import the tortoises from Tanzania. Since that time, however, poachers have begun smuggling the tortoises into the neighboring nation of Zambia. Although the pancake tortoise does not occur naturally in Zambia, it is now being sold internationally as "originating" there.

The sale of illegally harvested, smuggled rare turtles is big business. Tragically, that business will probably continue as long as there are customers willing to support it, no matter how strict the legal penalties may become. People who are interested in owning turtles should purchase only legal species, and only from dealers who can certify that the turtles were bred in captivity.

Indirect Destruction

As bad as overharvesting is for turtles, humans are doing even more harm to them indirectly, by destroying or changing their habitat. According to herpetologist and conservationist Michael W. Klemens, editor of *Turtle Conservation* (2000), "Loss and alteration of habitat are still the major causes of turtle decline around the world."

Everywhere in the world, wetlands are being drained, coastlines are being bulldozed, forests are being leveled, and swamps are being filled in to make room for housing developments, farms, and other human uses of the landscape. Nearly every species of turtle is affected by this activity. In addition to the simple loss of places to eat, live, and breed, turtles suffer the advance of the automobile. Each year, tens of thousands of slow-moving turtles are crushed under the wheels of cars and trucks. They also suffer from the animals that humans have introduced into their environments, including cats, dogs, pigs, and rats. These creatures do not necessarily eat turtles, but they eat turtle eggs.

Pollution is another human-caused threat to turtles. Because many species spend all or most of their time in water, they are vulnerable to water pollution, which can be especially concentrated in small, stagnant bodies of water like the ponds and swamps that many turtles inhabit. Another form of environmental pollution—garbage—is responsible for many turtle deaths. Leatherback turtles in particular are victims of this problem. The turtles' main food is jellyfish. A plastic bag floating in the water looks a lot like a jellyfish, but it is a lot less wholesome for the turtle. Dead leatherbacks have been found washed up on beaches, their intestines packed with plastic. Hawksbills and other marine turtles also suffer from plastic pollution.

One widespread threat to sea turtles is a contagious viral disease called fibropapillomatosis (FP), which causes tumors on the eyes, skin, and internal organs of sick turtles. FP has been known since the 1930s, but since the 1980s it has been spreading at a faster rate through sea turtle populations. Although the causes of FP are complex and not yet fully understood, there are signs that it may be linked to toxic outbreaks of marine algae. These outbreaks typically occur where the water is polluted by fertilizer, sewage, and certain kinds of industrial chemicals.

Tens of thousands of turtles are accidental victims of the fishing industry. Nets and lines studded with hooks often trail for dozens of miles behind industrial fishing vessels. The fishers may be trying to catch high-profit tuna or swordfish, but the nets and lines inevitably capture many other, unwanted animals. The

THE METAL GRATE OF THIS TURTLE EXCLUSION DEVICE (TED) LETS TRAPPED SEA TURTLES ESCAPE FROM A TRAWL USED TO CATCH SHRIMP.

fishing industry's term for these accidental victims is bycatch. Often the bycatch includes sea turtles, which become entangled in the nets or lines and drown. The situation of leatherbacks in the Pacific is particularly desperate. James R. Spotila, a founder of the International Sea Turtle Society and the author of *Sea Turtles* (2004), has reported that one leatherback nesting site in Mexico alone saw a drop from 70,000 turtles in 1982 to fewer than 250 in 1998.

Hope for the Future

The news about turtles is not all negative. There have been some victories in the battle to save turtles. The Kemp's ridley sea turtle, for example, used to be the most endangered marine

THE ARRIBADA IS THE NAME FOR THE MASS NESTING OF TURTLES, SUCH AS THE RIDLEY SEA TURTLES SHOWN HERE. THE GOVERNMENT OF COSTA RICA HOPES THAT A BALANCE OF HARVESTING AND PROTECTION WILL PRESERVE THE TURTLE POPULATION THAT HAS NESTED ON THIS BEACH FOR THOUSANDS OF YEARS.

turtle. This species nests on just one beach on the east coast of Mexico. Between the 1940s and the 1980s the number of females who came to the nesting site dropped from more than 40,000 to about 300. By 2004, however, that number had climbed back up to approximately 5,000, largely because of two strong conservation efforts.

One effort focused on protecting the actual nesting site. Volunteers monitored the beach during nesting season, watching for poachers and predators, while conservationists encouraged the Mexican government and people to value the turtles and their nests as a precious ecological asset. The other effort was aimed at reducing the bycatch of Kemp's ridleys and other sea turtles, which were being swept up in large numbers by vessels fishing for shrimp in the Gulf of Mexico. Environmental and conservation groups succeeded in convincing the U.S. Congress to pass a law requiring shrimp-fishing boats to use turtle excluding devices (TEDs) on their nets. The TEDs were metal grids designed to keep turtles from entering the large trawl nets. Despite years of furious opposition from U.S. shrimpers, and later from Asian nations that resisted pressure to adopt TEDs on their own shrimping boats, the devices are coming into wider use all the time. Sea turtle deaths are down in areas where they are used.

A different conservation approach is being tried for the olive ridley sea turtle. At Ostional in Costa Rica, one of the turtle's major nesting sites, local people have for centuries harvested turtle eggs. In 1983 the Costa Rican government established a wildlife refuge at Ostional. A few years later it started allowing the legal harvest of a certain percentage of the eggs each year. Conservationists do not yet know whether the Ostional project will control egg poaching in the long term. It is also too soon to tell whether the harvest will prove to be sustainable—that is, whether the olive ridley population will remain stable as more generations of eggs are harvested.

Sea turtle conservation has received considerable public attention. Ecotourism firms now conduct tours so that people can witness the nesting of sea turtles or even take part in beach patrols to protect the eggs and hatchlings. Dozens of other, less well-known turtle species could benefit from similar help. Turtle conservationists point out, however, that many turtles benefit from small-scale, local projects carried out by individuals and communities. Wetland protection, pollution control, and the creation of turtle tunnels under busy roadways may do much to help some common but threatened species. Other turtles will, perhaps, be saved only by the intervention of governments willing to pass and then enforce strict conservation laws. In the meantime, turtle ranching is on the rise, especially in Asia. Some experts think that the increased ranching of commercially desirable species such as softshells and river turtles will reduce the pressure on wild populations that are being overhunted.

"How tragic it would be for 200 million years of turtle evolution to all but disappear by the close of the twenty-first century," wrote Michael W. Klemens in *Turtle Conservation*. The obstacles facing turtles are formidable, but admiration for these ancient survivors runs deep. People have created the threats that currently endanger so many species of turtles, but working together, people may be able to steer turtles toward a more secure future.

Glossary

adapt—change or develop in ways that aid survival in the environment

ancestral—having to do with lines of descent or earlier forms

aquatic—spending all or part of the life cycle in water; used mainly for freshwater turtles; *see also* **marine**

carapace—upper part of a turtle's shell

chelonian—a turtle, or having to do with turtles

conservation—action or movement aimed at preserving wildlife or its habitat

cryptodire—turtle that draws its head straight back into its shell

ectothermic—cold-blooded, or lacking a means of producing and maintaining body heat; body temperature depends on environmental conditions

estivation—period of inactivity to survive the heat or drought of summer

evolve—to change over time; evolution is the pattern of new species, or types of plants and animals, emerging from old ones

extinct—no longer existing, died out

habitat—type of environment in which an animal lives

herpetology—scientific study of reptiles, including turtles

hibernation—period of inactivity to survive the cold of winter

longevity—length of life; often refers to long lives

marine—having to do with, or living in, salt water

metabolism—chemical processes by which an animal uses energy and maintains or builds tissue

paleontologist—scientist who practices paleontology, the study of ancient and extinct life forms, usually by examining fossil remains

plastron—lower part of a turtle's shell

pleurodire—turtle that tucks its head under its shell by bending its neck sharply to one side

scutes—scales or plates that make up the outer layer of a turtle's shell

terrapin—term sometimes used in North America for edible turtles or for the diamondback terrapin

terrestrial—spending all of the life cycle on land

tortoise—member of a family of land-dwelling turtles

Turtle Families Checklist

Families	Pelomedusidae (African mud turtles)
	Podocnemididae (South American and Malagasy river turtles)
	Chelidae (Australo-American side-neck turtles)
Suborder	Cryptodira (hidden-necks)
Families	Chelydridae (snapping turtles)
	Platysternidae (big-headed turtle)
	Cheloniidae (sea turtles other than leatherback)
	Dermochelyidae (leatherback sea turtle)
	Trionychidae (soft-shelled turtles)
	Carettochelyidae (pig-nose turtle)
	Dermatemydidae (Central American river turtle)
	Kinosternidae (mud and musk turtles)
	Emydidae (pond turtles)
	Bataguridae (Asian and American river turtles)
	Testudinidae (tortoises)

*This system of turtle classification is used by many herpetologists. Some scientists, though, favor alternate systems of classification with fewer families, or more, than are shown here.

Further Research

Books for Young People

Dennard, Deborah. *Turtles*. Chanhassen, MN: NorthWord, 2003.

Devaux, Bernard and Bernard de Wetter. *On the Trail of Sea Turtles*. Hauppauge, NY: Barron's, 2000.

Palika, Liz. *Turtles and Tortoises for Dummies*. New York: Hungry Minds, 2001.

Rhodes, Mary Jo and David Hall. *Sea Turtles*. New York: Children's Press, 2005.

Taylor, Barbara. *Turtles and Tortoises*. London: Lorenz, 2004.

Vrbova, Zuza. *Turtles*. Philadelphia: Chelsea House, 1998.

Videos and DVDs

Alligators and Crocodiles, Turtles and Tortoises. PBS Nature DVD, n.d.

Journey of the Loggerhead. Environmental Media Corp, 2004.

Sea Turtle Adventures. HBO Kids Video, 1997.

Sea Turtles. Vestron Video, 1998.

Web Sites

Some useful Web sites about turtles are listed here. Since this book was written, some of these sites may have changed, moved to new addresses, or gone out of existence. New sites may now be available.

http://www.kidskonnect.com/Turtles/TurtlesHome.html
> This kid-friendly site is a link to dozens of turtle-related pages that cover such topics as species identification and conservation.

http://www.junglewalk.com/video/Turtle-movie.htm
> This site offers eighty video clips of turtles in action, featuring many different species and habitats.

http://www.seaworld.org/infobooks/SeaTurtle/home.html
> Seaworld's educational Web site has a well-illustrated overview of facts about sea turtles.

http://animaldiversity.ummz.umich.edu/site/accounts/information/Testudines.html
> The University of Michigan Museum of Zoology maintains the Animal Diversity Web, with this set of pages on turtles and tortoises.

http://www.nmfs.noaa.gov/pr/species/turtles/
> This U.S. National Marine Fisheries Service page is a good place to start for information on the conservation of sea turtles in the United States.

http://tolweb.org/Testudines/14861

The Tree of Life Web project has a good page on turtle evolution and biology, with links to additional resources.

http://www.chelonian.org/

The Chelonian Research Foundation is an international group devoted to the study and protection of turtles; its Web page gives access to many articles in its Turtle and Tortoise Newsletter.

http://emys.geo.orst.edu/

This World Turtle Database is useful for identifying species and also for locating information about conservation efforts.

Bibliography

These books were especially useful to the author in researching this volume.

Alderton, David. *Turtles and Tortoises of the World*. New York: Facts On File, 2002.

Bonin, Franck, et al. Translated by Peter C.H. Pritchard. *Turtles of the World*. Baltimore: Johns Hopkins University Press, 2006.

Chambers, Paul. *A Sheltered Life*. New York: Oxford University Press, 2006.

Klemens, Michael W., editor. *Turtle Conservation*. Washington, D.C.: Smithsonian Institution Press, 2000.

Orenstein, Ronald. *Turtles, Tortoises, and Terrapins: Survivors in Armor*. Buffalo, NY: Firefly, 2001.

Spotila, James R. *Sea Turtles: A Complete Guide to Their Biology, Behavior, and Conservation*. Baltimore: Johns Hopkins University Press, 2004.

Witherington, Blair. *Sea Turtles: An Extraordinary History of Some Uncommon Turtles*. St. Paul, MN: Voyageur, 2006.

Index

Page numbers in **boldface** are illustrations.

About the Author

Rebecca Stefoff has written numerous nonfiction books for readers of all ages. Among her books on scientific topics are several other volumes in the AnimalWays series, including *Horses*, *Tigers*, *Chimpanzees*, and *Deer*. Stefoff has also written for Benchmark Books' Family Trees series, which explores the relationships among different groups of living things. She is the author of *Charles Darwin and the Evolution Revolution* (Oxford, 1996) and appeared in the A&E *Biography* episode on Darwin and his work. Find out more about the author and her books at www.rebeccastefoff.com.